JUST SAY YES!
Chronicle of a Stroke Survivor

Karen Franzenburg

JUST SAY YES!

Copyright © 2018 by Karen Franzenburg
All rights reserved

ISBN: 978-0-578-21126-8

Published by Karen Franzenburg, San Jose, California, 95118.

Printed in the United States of America.

PUBLISHER'S NOTE: This book is based on the author's own, personal experiences.

Cover photograph and all photographs by Karen Franzenburg except for photos on pages 24 and 25 by Wm. Irvine

To order additional books go to: **http://www.LuLu.com, Amazon.com or Barnesandnoble.com**

Email: franzenburgk@gmail.com

Little White Feather

Dedication

To my family and friends. I sincerely want to thank them and the medical personnel for helping me through this very difficult time in my life.

Acknowledgements

My sincerest gratitude goes to all those who encouraged me to write a letter to my stroke and to write this book. Thank you to Luanna Leisure for working with me on editing and through the publishing process.

This is a chronicle of the events of my battle with a stroke. I was informed and I fought hard. Not everyone is affected by a stroke in the same way. Symptoms may differ and not everyone can follow the same medical procedures. The health care provider and the stroke patient must consider what is right for the patient. This book is not a guide for what an individual should do medically, it is a book about my personal experience.

To everyone who reads my story, please take the time to learn the symptoms of a stroke. If you experience any of them, do not hesitate to call 911 or have someone assist you to do so.

If you have an opportunity to go to a seminar that includes talks about strokes, do yourself a favor and go. I did and I am so thankful I took the time. It may have saved my life.

Something's Wrong

I reach for the alarm. I am thinking about how hot it may get today. The early Sunday morning sunshine is peering through the sheer curtains. My friend, the hummingbird, is outside the sliding glass door. I can hear the flutter of his wings. I pull the curtains open. Watching this beautiful bird lifts my spirits and brightens my day. I open the door in hopes of cooling the house down.

I turn to head toward the hall. My ankle suddenly twists. I feel a couple of seconds of confusion. I wonder why this is happening. I didn't trip on anything. I take a couple of more steps and walk into the hall. Thoughts are going through my head. My early morning ritual is about to take a surprising turn.

"This is the moment I meet you, Mr. Stroke." I am vulnerable. "You are a stranger to me."

I am approaching unfamiliar territory. A feeling as if the floor is moving comes over me. I question if we are having the beginning of an earthquake. I feel unsteady.

"You take me under your wing gently the first second or two. Now you give me a turn. What power I let you have."

I lose my balance.

"You, Mr. Stroke, are beginning to control me. My leg starts to feel like Jell-O. You come closer, more intimate. You give me a push in a different direction. It makes me feel insecure, frightened and in danger. I cannot get out of your grasp.

I am swaying. What is happening? The more I try to gain control, the more power you suck out of me. My right leg is feeling heavy and it is dragging now. I almost fall. I need help to fight you."

I scream out, "Help, Bill, help me! Something is wrong, my leg is giving out."

He is asleep. He mumbles, "What, what?"

"You are still commanding my body to stay with you, Mr. Stroke. I am fighting your all-consuming grasp."

"Bill, help. My leg is not working. I am going to fall. Something is happening to my leg. Something strange is happening. I don't feel right. Help me."

Bill is grabbing me. Helping me to the toilet seat, the closest place to set me down. He is getting my blood tester to see if I am having a low blood sugar attack.

My sugar tested fine.

"I'm calling 911," he says. He hands me the phone.

"When the operator answers tell her what is happening. I will be right back I want to go unlock the front door. You may be having a stroke."

"In the meantime you, Mr. Stroke, have a strong hold on me. I feel your giant weighted grasp on my right leg."

I tell the operator what is happening. "Please hurry, I think I am having a stroke."

"Can you tell me what symptoms you're having?"

"I am losing control of my right leg and it's feeling heavy."

"They are on the way," she says. "Try to remain as calm as possible."

"Where are they?" I ask.

I try to get up. "I can't get up," I tell her. "I'm scared."

"They are on their way. Is someone with you?"

"Yes," I reply.

"You're going to be in good hands. They should be pulling up now."

"They are here," Bill shouts to me.

I tell the operator, "They are here."

"You are in good hands. You take care."

We hang up.

"She is in here," I hear Bill tell the paramedics.

"By now you, stroke, are controlling my right leg. Stroke, you are so powerful. You want me to give in, don't you?"

My leg feels so heavy. I can hardly move it or my toes. It is starting to feel heavier.

"Dear God, am I really having a stroke? I won't, I won't give in. I will give it my all. I will fight you."

The EMTs put me into the ambulance. They take my vitals and ask me questions. It seems like they are taking a long time. I hear the siren and we are on our way to the hospital.

"Am I having a stroke?" I ask.

"You are going to be okay. They know exactly what to do. You're going to the best stroke center. They will see if you are having one or if something else is going on. We are almost there. You will be in good hands. There are specialists waiting to see you. We are sending them some of the information they need to know about you right now. It won't be long."

A few minutes go by.

"We are turning into the emergency entrance of the hospital now," the EMT says to me.

Emergency Room Nine

A quick lift onto a hospital gurney takes me into another turn of events. I am being wheeled into the emergency room. I hear, "Brain attack emergency room nine. Brain attack emergency room nine." I remember they wheeled me into room nine. This is happening so quickly.

Now my right leg will not budge. I can't even get my toes to wiggle. My leg feels like something is sitting on it. It is heavy. I think I am having a stroke. I am almost certain of it now.

"You, stroke, are not letting me go. You want me. You are using me."

The stroke team is examining me. A man in a white coat is smiling down at me. I heard him say he is a neurologist. He is asking me questions.

"Do you know where you are? What time did your symptoms start?"

It sounds like a game of fifty questions. I hear one question after another.

"What time did your symptoms start? Can you tell me what happened?" I hear the doctor ask.

"I woke up at 6:00 a.m. and walked to open the sliding glass door. I turned around to walk to the hall and my ankle twisted. A couple of seconds later I took two or three steps, shrugging off what just happened. Then as I turned to go down the hall toward the bathroom my right leg gave way. I started to lose my balance. I called out to Bill. Things progressed and Bill dialed 911."

"So, a little after 6:00 a.m. this all started?" The doctor wanted confirmation again.

"Yes."

I am feeling a bit of confusion, a slight inability to comprehend things right now.

"It started right after 6:00 a.m. when I got up. The sliding glass door is only about three or four steps from my bed. It didn't take more than a minute to open that door and take a couple of steps and that's when it started."

"It is important we know when this all started," the neurologists says. He looks at Bill who is sitting in the corner of the room. I guess he did not put full trust in my recall.

"I heard her wake up and I looked at the clock. It was 6:00 a.m.," Bill answered.

Then I hear the doctor say, "We need a CAT scan ASAP." The doctor is standing near me. "I am going to hold your leg up, when I let it go, try to hold it up as long as you can." He holds it up and lets go. It crashes down like a two ton weight. He tries that procedure again. The result is the same. I couldn't hold it up.

"I am really trying, but it is a dead weight," I tell the doctor.

"Yes, I understand," he replies.

He looks at Bill then the nurse. An orderly comes in. "Take her to CAT scan now," the doctor orders.

"We are taking you for your scan. It shouldn't take long," the orderly tells me.

A short time later they wheel me into the CAT scan department through the double door entry.

"Brain attack," the nurse says when they wheel me into the CAT scan room. I can hear the technician tell a lady in the waiting room, "This is an emergency. You will have to wait awhile."

I heard the lady answer, "I understand."

They take one set of scans then hook me up to an IV line.

"We need another one with contrast," the neurologist says.

They finish scanning.

The neurologist is in the room with what looks like other doctors. They are viewing the scan. The neurologist comes into the scanning room. "I will review these with the team and come back to ER. You can take her back."

The orderly and nurse wheel me back to ER.

I see the neurologist coming into the ER area.

"The lab tests just came," I hear a nurse say as she shows the paperwork to the neurologist.

It seems like a couple of minutes go by. The neurologist comes in. "You are having a stroke. You just have a short time frame for me to offer you a clot buster medication. It may or may not help. If it does, it can possibly give you a chance to prevent further damage and maybe reverse what is happening. I do have to let you know that the stroke could cause permanent damage or worse."

"What are the possible side effects of that IV?" I ask him.

I am feeling half out of it. One minute it seems my brain is functioning. The next I feel confused.

"If you take the IV it can have serious consequences. You can bleed out. You could hemorrhage and die."

"What? I could die! Bill did you hear that? I could hemorrhage or die."

"The stroke could kill you," the neurologist tells me. "So, you have to make up your mind. It is up to you. I cannot tell you what to decide. You have a few minutes left to make your decision. I cannot give the IV to you without your permission. We need at least thirty minutes to administer the IV, because it has to drip into you slowly. You have less than twenty more minutes to make your decision. I have to step out for a minute. I will be back soon. You can let the nurse know if you want the medication."

"Just Say Yes!"

I can see the neurologist talking to another doctor, and they look my way. I see the other doctor shake his head and look at Bill.

The other doctor comes in. He introduces himself to Bill. "Has she decided yet?" He asks. I guess he thinks I am not able to speak.

"I need a few minutes. This is scary," I say.

"You only have a few more minutes and your window to have the IV medication is gone," the neurologist says.

I remember his face. He was at the stroke and A-Fib seminar Bill and I went to a couple of weeks ago.

Bill looked at him and said, "I can't tell you to do it because we aren't married. I keep telling her to say yes. I'm not getting anywhere."

The doctor shakes his head. "I see." He looks at the nurse. "Are the lines ready?"

"Yes, we have it all set if she makes the decision."

"Okay," he says and leaves the room. I see him talking to the previous stroke doctor.

"You better not screw around," Bill says. "Get that medicine. You don't want this to possibly progress. You have to tell them now. You can't move your leg. If you wait, you can get worse."

Bill keeps telling me, "Remember the seminar that we went to a couple of weeks ago on strokes and A-Fib. Remember they said it's important to get the IV in time."

I hear Bill say, "Get the medicine now. Say yes, say yes."

My brain is confused. I hear him, but it seems garbled in my head.

"You, Mr. Stroke, are messing with my brain and thought process."

I am trying to move my toes. I guess I am hoping they will move and it will be over. They won't budge.

"I am trying to fight you, with all I have in me, Mr. Stroke."

I hear Bill say, "Take the medicine. You don't want to get worse. Say yes. Just say yes!"

I could hear him better now. My thought process was clearer at this moment in time.

"Okay, do it, give me the clot buster," I tell the nurse.

"Did I hear you say you want the clot buster IV?"

I shake my head in a yes motion.

"I will get the neurologist," she replies.

The neurologist comes in. "I hear you want the medicine."

"Yes," I say.

"You are just under the cut off. Ten more minutes and we could not start it for you. Let's get this going," he says to the nurse.

He directs the dance with speed and expertise. They start giving me the clot buster IV. I am scared.

I am getting the IV medication. They finally finish it in the time allowed.

"All done," the nurse says. "I will be with you until the team comes from Neuro ICU. They will take you to a special unit and explain everything that will happen in the next few hours."

The neurologist leaves the room.

Bill comes over to my bedside. "I am so glad you made that decision."

"It is frightening to hear that either way the medicine or the stroke could kill me. That took a few minutes to sink in and I finally came to the conclusion that, if it's my time to go, it's my time. At least the medicine may give me a chance at stopping the stroke damage or minimizing it."

A nurse and orderly enter the room.

"We need to take her to Neuro Intensive Care now," they tell Bill. "You can come up for a few minutes, so you know where she will be and get her belongings. Then you can go home. We will take good care of her. Someone will be watching her the whole time she is in there."

I am being wheeled into a room with a glass partition. There is a nurse sitting at a small desk behind the glass.

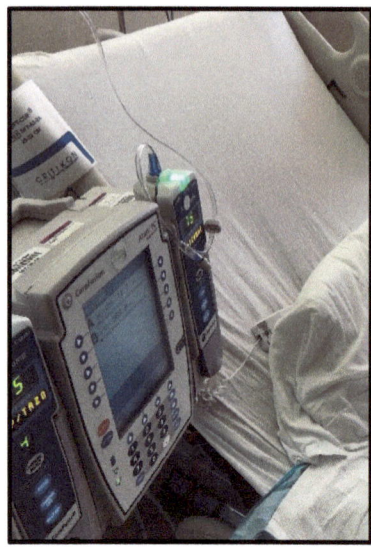

They have me moved onto a special bed with lots of controls and beeping machines on both sides.

Bill says, "Do you want me to stay with you for a few minutes?"

"No, I will have someone with me. They know what to look for if I have a problem, and they can call you. You need to go relax and rest."

After saying our goodbyes, Bill starts to leave to go home for some rest.

On his way out he tells the nurse, "Okay, I'll go, but you make sure to call me if there are any changes."

"We will monitor her the whole time she is in here."

"Don't worry I am safe and in good hands," I reassure him.

Bill leaves.

The nurse begins to talk to me. "You may start bleeding from your mouth or nose and that is a normal thing. We will be questioning you every fifteen minutes for the next hour. After that, every half hour for the next twenty-three hours. We have to keep you awake. It is very important we do this. We will be asking you questions to keep listening to your speech. We have to ask you to move your arms and to swallow. We will be watching you closely to be sure you're not having signs of another stroke occurrence. Do you understand?"

"Yes," I reply.

"Meanwhile you, Stroke, are getting a taste of my powerful choice. The IV medication is circulating inside my body. Soon you will feel it attack you. I imagine it is finding its way to my brain right now."

I say a quick silent prayer. "Please, God, give me the strength to fight this."

The clot buster is swimming in my veins. I am praying it safely clears any clot in my brain.

I brush aside the negative thoughts and momentary fears. I will fight this. I have to fight this.

The next ten hours are critical. The staff in Neuro Intensive Care watch for the signs. They tell me that the clot buster they gave me is the most powerful one they have.

I can't feel anything but dead weight in my right leg and foot.

"You are like a giant vice, Mr. Stroke. I can't even get a little toe movement."

This is a frightening experience.

The ten hours of critical bleed watch is over. Now they tell me the next thirteen hours will be more of the same. They watch for anymore stroke symptoms.

I pass the next thirteen hours with no indication of another stroke.

The doctor ordered another CAT scan. They want to check things out.

I am being taken for another CAT scan. They need to check for any bleeding in the brain. If it is clear, they will do an MRI. After the scan they take me into a room to wait. The results of the CAT scan show it to be clear. I am told I have to wait 24 more hours to take the MRI.

Fighting to Survive

The next day they take me down for an MRI. Everything comes out okay.

"I am fighting to survive you, Mr. Stroke. This is one of the hardest fights of my life. I am determined you will not win."

I struggle with every ounce of strength I have. For two more days I try desperately to move my leg, but to no avail. Then I manage to wiggle a toe a tiny bit. I was elated to say the least. This may mean I will be okay. I push the call button to tell someone.

A voice comes on the speaker, "Do you need something?"

"My toe moved. I got my toe to move," I tell her.

A nurse came to check up on me.

"See it moved. It moved," I exclaim.

"We will let the doctors know. Good for you." She leaves to deliver the news.

The neurologist comes in a few minutes later. He sees my toe movement.

"That's a good sign. We can transfer you down the hall to another room and out of this area for now."

I am being released from Neuro ICU into the other room.

I started trying to get my leg to move. I got my knee to rise just a little with the help of my hands. At least it moved about the width of my finger. I struggled to try. I know now I need help.

The neurologist comes to see me the next morning and tells me I will be transferred to the stroke rehab hospital later today.

I am taken over to the intensive stroke rehab center.

After getting checked in and settled into my room, I get to have a lunch.

They bring in the tray. The aides prop me up in the bed with a tray. Thank God my arms are mobile. I ate and buzzed the desk to let them know I had finished eating.

An aide came to collect the tray.

I am telling the aide, "I got my toes to move. I will get to walk again."

"You may or may not be able to walk again," she says.

"Don't say that to me. I will walk again. I will."

She replies, "That is a good attitude. You need to think like that to get through this."

She leaves the room.

One morning after aides put pillows behind me so I could sit up, I decide to try and bend my leg. I put both of my hands under my knee and told myself I can do it. I keep at it. It is taking all the strength I can muster to try to pull my knee up. By early evening I got it up. What a triumph. I buzzed the desk. The nurse came in and I told her what I did.

"Good. I will let the doctor know," the nurse says.

She is happy for me. She made a call to the neurologist, and he directed her to talk to the therapists.

The nurse tells me the therapists will be coming to interview me. They will test me and then set up schedules for therapy sessions.

The next morning a nurse came in. She posted the appointment on the bulletin board next to the bathroom door.

"Make sure you're ready a few minutes earlier than the times that are written here. The therapists do not like to have patients come late to their sessions. Someone will come to wheel you to the appointments."

After a day or two I ask the physical therapist if I can try to sit up in the chair. They assist me to the chair and make sure I am okay. I combed my hair.

17

Then they helped me to stand up. I take a couple of steps with a physical therapist on each side helping to hold me up. They strap a thick belt around my waist. It looks like the ones Kung Fu guys you see in karate movies wear. Only mine is white with yellow fluorescent stripes.

One of them tells me, "We have to use this when we get you up to stand or walk. We don't want you to fall."

I reached a point that I felt secure and told them I no longer needed that belt. They stood at my sides and let go of the belt. I found out quickly I better follow their instructions.

I am beginning to see the after-effects of the stroke. It is amazing how the different therapies made me aware of the problems I would have if I went home too early.

"Gradually you, Mr. Stroke, let a little of your grip give way."

I begin walking with assistance from my bed to the bathroom in the corner of my room. My balance was messed up. I had to admit to myself I needed their help.

Later that day the physical therapist asked me if I wanted to try to take a shower. She told me we had to walk to the end of the hall where the showers were.

"Are you kidding me? Yes! Yes! It will be wonderful. Can we go now?"

"Give me a minute to go get towels and bring your clean clothes down there."

"Okay," I answer.

She returns. "Let's go," The therapist says as she helps me.

We head to the shower.

"I can do it. I don't need you to help me," I tell her as we enter the shower room area.

"I have to stay here. I will sit outside. Let me know if you need help. Hospital rules. You have to promise me, if you start to feel weak or dizzy, you will sit down on the shower bench and tell me."

"I promise I will."

"You have to be able to show me you can turn the water on and off before you get to take a shower. I know this seems ridiculous to you, but I have to document the things you can and cannot do. We need to know if you will need assistance at home and how much."

"I know how to take a shower. I can handle it. If I get tired I will sit in the shower chair. We have one at home. I had it when my mom stayed with us, and Bill will be with me until I know I am okay."

"Well, just turn the faucet on and adjust the temperature. Then turn it off so I can document it."

"Okay."

I follow her instructions.

"Okay, go ahead. I will be here, if you need me."

I close the curtains and hand her my robe. I turn the water on. This is heaven. I start to feel tears well in my eyes as the warm water flows over me. Wow, I walked all the way down the hall. I can talk, walk, eat, and now I get to give myself a shower. Tears are now flowing down my cheeks. I sniffle.

"Are you okay?" The therapist asks.

"I am. I tell you this is heaven. I never knew a shower could feel so good."

"We hear that a lot," she replied.

I finished, and she handed me the towel. I moved to a chair near where my clothes were. I pulled the curtain and put on my clothes. Then she helped me get a mirror, and I combed my hair. I am feeling tired.

They warned me I could get tired quickly and to rest when I felt tired. They told me that is normal after a stroke and may continue for some time and to just give in to it and rest.

I let the therapist know I felt exhausted. This is the most I have accomplished in days. We headed back to my room.

"I will bring your things back to you as soon as I know you are in your bed."

I made it back.

She returned my personal things. "Okay, you rest and I will see you tomorrow." I could hear her say, "You did good today."

Believe me, this was a big day for me. A huge day. The beginning of getting my life back. I closed my eyes to get some rest before dinner time.

"Sure, challenges are definitely ahead, but I am beating you, Mr. Stroke. I know I am."

I have occupational therapy, speech therapy and physical therapy every day. I also had meetings with a neuropsychologist.

I'm Winning

"Yes, inch by inch I fight you, Mr. Stroke. Day after day I fight your grip."

Much to the doctors and nurses surprise, I am able to walk with the help of a cane. They are not certain how long I will need it, but they want me to use it to prevent falling. I have some issues, however, thanks to the experts here, I am aware of my strengths and weaknesses. There are things I have to work on. At least I know that it is important to be aware and careful of my surroundings. It does take time to adjust. Things happen a bit slower for me as far as my motor skills.

"However, Mr. Stroke, you did not win this battle. You will not win the next or the next."

I had to pass a series of tests. Each division of therapy had to sign a release stating I passed their tests. I worked hard and passed every one of them. I have to go to occupational therapy, speech therapy and physical therapy for a few more months on an outpatient basis.

My neuropsychologist suggested I attend outside group therapy sessions. Early on, she saw me taking notes about my experience. "Do me a favor, write a letter to your stroke," she said. I wrote the letter and that led me to write this book.

I feel pretty normal. I can hardly wait to go home.

The doctors and neurologists say I am fortunate to have such a good recovery. The staff say it is a miracle I am doing so well. They are amazed at my determination to get well and tell me my attitude really helped me.

I am warned that I could experience another stroke. They tell me the chances are higher once you have had a prior stroke.

"I am told that you, Mr. Stroke, are called a mild stroke."

It is something I do not ever want to experience again. I intend to take good care of myself.

I told them I am lucky. I had superb care and I prayed for the strength to fight. I put it in the hands of God.

Bill asked the doctor, "What would have happened, if she had stayed asleep and not woke up?"

"We would not have known when the symptoms started. That is one crucial piece of information. We need to know the onset time since the medication has a timing issue. She was very lucky she woke up when she did and that she qualified for the IV and was able to receive it in time. Her determination to get well helped her fight her way to getting better. She is one lucky lady. No telling what might have happened if she did not wake up when she did."

"Yes, it could have been a lot worse. Thank you for helping me pull through this," I tell the doctor. He smiled and left my room.

I thank God for giving me the strength to face the physical and mental trials of this experience.

The staff placed a banner across my doorway and gave me a t-shirt that said, Graduated from Intensive Stroke Rehab. We all shared some cake.

The therapist wheels me out to the elevator. Everyone waves and smiles. One of the other stroke patients sat in his wheel chair and tried to lift his arm to wave to me. He said, "You're going home! Good for you!"

I smiled and nodded yes. Our eyes connected as one stroke patient to another. I could see hope in his eyes.

"Mr. Stroke, you showed me that I am strong. I can survive. I can dance to a new life. I can adapt. I feel blessed to be accounted worthy for the opportunity to enjoy the rest of my life."

Author

Karen Franzenburg

During the stroke and my recovery I felt as if I had been in a dream state. I was not frightened but I had a determined attitude and inner strength. It felt like my soul knew everything was going to be okay. In retrospect, I felt I had a purpose in life and part of that was to complete this book so others could be more informed. I wanted to increase their awareness of the importance of acknowledging stroke symptoms and getting immediate help at the onset.

I enjoy writing. Some of my short stories and poems have been published in California Writers Club-South Bay Branch newsletters, the American Poetry Anthology and other anthology publications. I have won critics' choice and several awards in literary competitions.

I am an award winning artist and photographer. I love to photograph landscapes, nature and wildlife. I am active in the artistic and literary communities belonging to the California Writers-South Bay Branch, San Jose Poetry, Willow Glen Poetry, Campbell Artist Guild and The National League of American Pen Women.

I feel fortunate to have survived the stroke and through excellent therapy I am able to continue my various artistic interests.

www.ingramcontent.com/pod-product-compliance
Lightning Source LLC
Chambersburg PA
CBHW041523090426

42737CB00037B/22